LEGO STAR WARS™

AWESOME VEHICLES

Written by
Simon Hugo

CONTENTS

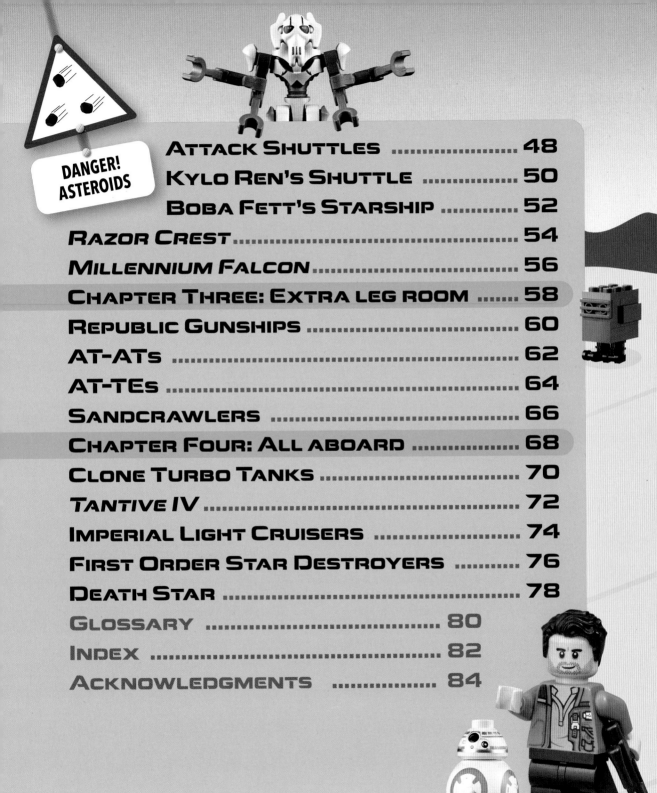

DANGER!
ASTEROIDS

INTRODUCING A GALAXY OF VEHICLES

WITH RESISTANCE HERO POE DAMERON

What's the best ship in the galaxy? It's my own T-70 X-wing starfighter, *Black One*, of course! I don't plan to part with my X-wing any time soon. So, what is the best galactic ride for you? Find out over the pages that follow.

I'll guide you through some great vehicles, from a small speeder bike to the biggest battle station. If you can't find something to meet your needs here, then you might just have to build your own!

Travel safe and may the Force be with you.

Poe

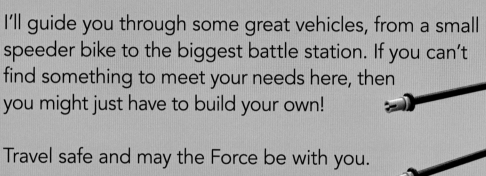

Hey, BB-8! Ready to see the coolest craft in the galaxy?

Poe's droid, BB-8

Landing strut retracts during takeoff

BAY DOORS OPEN!

MIND THE FORCE FIELD!

BB-8 travels here

Maintenance engineer

Only Poe's T-70 X-wing comes in these cool colors!

Boarding ladder

Maintenance sled

Everything's A-OK in an A-wing!

USE BOONTA BRAND
PODRACER FUEL

IT'S A
BLAST!

CHAPTER ONE

GOING SOLO

When it's just you and your droid, these compact craft are the vehicles you're looking for! From starfighters to ski speeders, the vehicles in this section have just one seat. They still pack in plenty of other features for your solo adventures.

SPEEDER
BIKE LANE

**RECENT
DESTINATIONS:**

DANTOOINE

DEATH STAR

SECRET BASE
(YAVIN 4)

SELECT AN OPTION BELOW
TO START YOUR JOURNEY

BEGIN VOICE
NAVIGATION

USE
FORCE

001138

X-WING SATNAV

A-WING STARFIGHTERS

1,300 KPH ZONE

If you're looking for a grade-A vehicle, you can't do much better than an A-wing starfighter. Much loved by rebels and Resistance pilots alike, its simple wedge-shaped design forgoes any fancy details in favor of being fast, fast, fast!

This ship is awesome with a capital "A!"

Resistance pilot Snap Wexley

Stabilizer fins for flying in planetary atmospheres

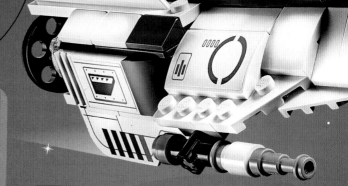

MISSION LOG

BATTLE OF ENDOR
Classic RZ-1 A-wings played an important role in the destruction of the second Death Star above the Forest Moon of Endor.

DEFENSE OF D'QAR
When the First Order attacked the planet D'Qar, RZ-2 A-wings went into battle. This gave other Resistance ships time to escape.

ALTERNATIVE VIEW

Quick-escape cockpit

Powerful twin thrusters

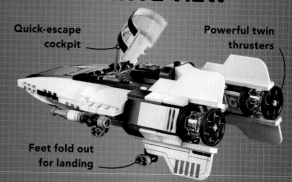

Feet fold out for landing

OPTIONAL EXTRAS

Most A-wings have powerful defensive shields. You can strip these out to go even faster—if you dare!

Laser cannons need regular maintenance

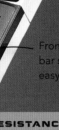

RESISTANCE A-WING STARFIGHTER

WHAT TO WEAR

Many A-wing pilots wear distinctive cheek-hugging helmets that do not require a chinstrap. It's a classic look, and handy for any aliens who don't have chins.

Front tow bar slot for easy parking

NEED TO KNOW

Model: RZ-2 A-wing Interceptor

Length: 7.7 m (25 ft)

Top speed: 1,350 kph (838 mph)

Weapons: Laser cannons, missile launchers

Made by: Kuat Systems Engineering

[OVERDUE!]

Dear Pilot,

Your RZ-2 A-wing Interceptor has been recorded traveling at 1,350 kph in a 1,300 kph zone. You must pay 1,000 New Republic Credits within 10 days of this notice or your vehicle will be seized and may be sold for scrap.

May the Force be with you,

The Republic Tribunal (Traffic Division)

A galaxy of color . . .

A-wing starfighter— also available in red!

B-WING STARFIGHTERS

B-wing starfighters have powerful weapons and special rotating cockpits. But their lack of speed made them unpopular with pilots, and most were stripped down for parts. For that reason, this ship is something of a collector's item in the New Republic era.

Ion cannon

ALTERNATIVE VIEW

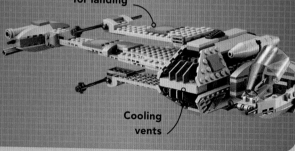

Wings fold flat for landing

Cooling vents

 ## NEED TO KNOW

Model: A/SF-01 B-wing starfighter

Length: 16.9 m (55 ft)

Top speed: 950 kph (590 mph)

Weapons: Laser cannons, ion cannon, proton torpedo launchers

Made by: Slayn & Korpil

AS USED BY ...

Hera Syndulla
This rebel pilot flew the first ever B-wing. It was a bright-orange prototype called the B6.

PROS AND CONS

IN A B-WING

Smaller wings fold out in battle mode

Blade-shaped main wing gives the ship its name

👍 Packed with more weapons than some larger ships.

👍 Great for a relaxed sight-seeing tour of the galaxy.

👎 Slow-moving compared to X-wings, Y-wings, and TIE fighters.

👎 Might not be able to keep up with friends driving faster ships.

- DON'T TOSS - YOUR B-WINGS!

🚀 + 🚀 + 🚀 = 🚀

Return your old B-wing parts to the Slayn & Korpil shipyard, and we will recycle them to make Resistance transport ships!

B-WING STARFIGHTER

Cockpit also serves as an escape pod

Rebel Gray Squadron pilot

Ten Numb
This brave member of Blue Squadron defeated two Star Destroyers in his B-wing.

To "B" or not to "B?" Now there's a question!

15

X-WING STARFIGHTERS

The iconic X-wing might just be the most famous starfighter in the galaxy, but is it the right ship for you? Well, if you're looking for speed, style, and a place to store your astromech, the answer is probably yes. If you want to be like Luke Skywalker, the answer is also yes!

Wings open for combat

Now available!

New

T-70 X-wing starfighter

Astromech droid connected to ship's systems

Luke Skywalker at the controls

One of four laser cannons

That "X" really hits the spot!

Wings also known as strike foils

SWAMP-PROOF YOUR X-WING WITH

DAGOBAH-BOG-BE-GONE

MASTER YODA SAYS: "A POWERFUL ALLY IT IS!"

MISSION LOG

BATTLE OF YAVIN
Luke Skywalker used the Force and a T-65 X-wing fighter to single-handedly blow up the first Death Star.

DOWNED ON DAGOBAH
Luke took his X-wing to Dagobah in search of Jedi Master Yoda, where it survived sinking in a swamp.

BATTLE OF TAKODANA
Resistance X-wings came to the rescue when the First Order attacked the planet Takodana in search of a map that led to Luke Skywalker.

Destroying the Death Star might chip your paintwork

LUKE SKYWALKER'S X-WING

NEED TO KNOW

Model: T-65 X-wing starfighter

Length: 13.4 m (44 ft)

Top speed: 1,050 kph (652 mph)

Weapons: Laser cannons, proton torpedo launchers

Made by: Incom Corporation

AS USED BY . . .

Luke Skywalker
From the Battle of Yavin to his secluded life on the planet Ahch-To, Luke was never far from a T-65 X-wing!

Biggs Darklighter
Luke's boyhood friend also grew up to be an X-wing pilot in the Rebellion's Red Squadron.

Poe Dameron
Who's this dashing guy? Why, it's only the ace pilot of the T-70 X-wing known as *Black One*!

RED SQUADRON X-CLUSIVE!

THIS CARD ENTITLES THE HOLDER TO A FREE X-WING WAX AND POLISH EVERY 100,000,000 KM. RED SQUADRON MEMBERS ONLY. ASTROMECH OIL BATHS NOT INCLUDED.

Y-WING STARFIGHTERS

If you love tinkering with machinery, a Y-wing is just the thing. Most early models have had their hull plating stripped away for easy access to their workings. The latest versions are actually built that way. This makes it easy to repair these sturdy starfighters.

Sensor dome

Rotating ion cannon

Resistance fighter Zorii Bliss

Astromech droid

MISSION LOG

BATTLE OF SCARIF
BTL Y-wings helped in this rebel mission to steal the Death Star plans from the Imperial archives on Scarif.

BATTLE OF EXEGOL
Poe's old pal Zorii Bliss flew her Y-wing with the Resistance in their final battle against the First Order.

DRIVER'S LICENSE

NAME:
Zorii Bliss

ADDRESS:
Spice Runners' Hideout, Kijimi

HEIGHT:
1.62 m
(5 ft 4 in)

ID PHOTO REJECTED!

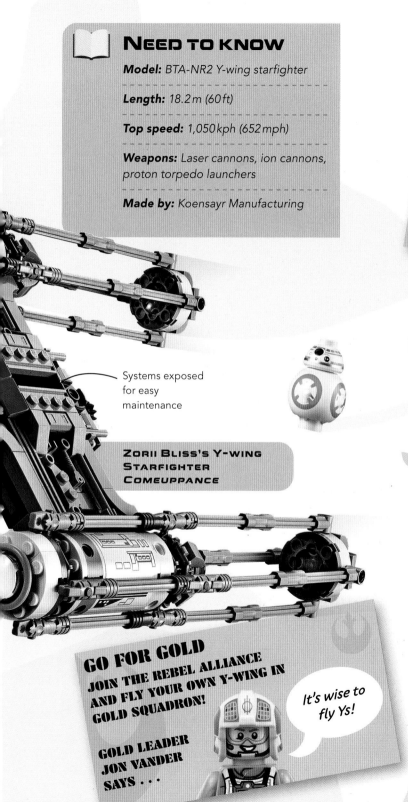

NEED TO KNOW

Model: BTA-NR2 Y-wing starfighter

Length: 18.2 m (60 ft)

Top speed: 1,050 kph (652 mph)

Weapons: Laser cannons, ion cannons, proton torpedo launchers

Made by: Koensayr Manufacturing

Systems exposed for easy maintenance

ZORII BLISS'S Y-WING STARFIGHTER COMEUPPANCE

WHY WALK when you can Y-WING?

Visit your nearest Y-wing dealer today!

"Y" fly anything else?

GOING GREEN?

Y-wings are built to last and mechanics can keep them in the skies for even longer. Definitely a sustainable choice!

GO FOR GOLD

JOIN THE REBEL ALLIANCE AND FLY YOUR OWN Y-WING IN GOLD SQUADRON!

GOLD LEADER JON VANDER SAYS . . .

It's wise to fly Ys!

PERFECT FOR . . .

Pilots looking for a ship that doesn't have many bells and whistles, but that can be customized time and again!

19

IMPERIAL TIE FIGHTERS

Say what you like about the Empire, but they knew how to make a starfighter. Named for their loud Twin Ion Engines, TIE fighters are designed not only to fight, but also to spread fear simply by roaring overhead. Do *not* get one of these if you want to make friends!

TRY BEFORE YOU FLY . . .

Not keen on hexagons? Get straight to the point with a Sith TIE fighter. Its triangular solar panels also come with a cool red trim!

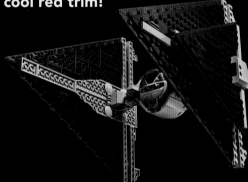

Performance
★★★★★

Handling
★★★★★

Usability
★★★★★

Overall
★★★★★

NEED TO KNOW

Model: *TIE/In space superiority starfighter*

- - - - - - - - - - - - - - - - - - -

Length: *7.2 m (24 ft)*

- - - - - - - - - - - - - - - - - - -

Top speed: *1,200 kph (746 mph)*

- - - - - - - - - - - - - - - - - - -

Weapons: *Laser cannons*

- - - - - - - - - - - - - - - - - - -

Made by: *Sienar Fleet Systems*

- You are invited to the -

Imperial Pilot's Annual Dinner

Free parking on the Death Star (Black TIE only)

I'd like to tie a knot in that TIE!

Small
cockpit

Laser
cannon

TIE FIGHTER

Side panels are
solar collectors

?? OPTIONAL EXTRAS

Available upgrades
for the TIE line include
faster-than-light drives
and mean-looking red
windows, as seen here
in Kylo Ren's TIE silencer.

TIE PILOT LOYALTY CARD

1 2 3 4 5

Blast three rebel ships and meet the Emperor!
Blast five and you <u>don't</u> have to meet the Emperor!

👕 WHAT TO WEAR

TIE fighters are *not*
built for comfort.
In fact, they don't
even have any
atmosphere!
You'll need
special breathing
gear to fly one
in space.

🌿 GOING GREEN?

*TIE fighters are surprisingly
environmentally friendly. Their large
solar panels use starlight to power
the engines and laser cannons.*

SOULLESS ONE

You don't need four arms to fly this starfighter, but it helps! Modified for the six-limbed cyborg General Grievous, its small cockpit is surrounded by heavily armored engines. Because Grievous sometimes used this ship for flying away from battle, it was also known as the *Spineless One*.

Lightsabers left at owner's risk!

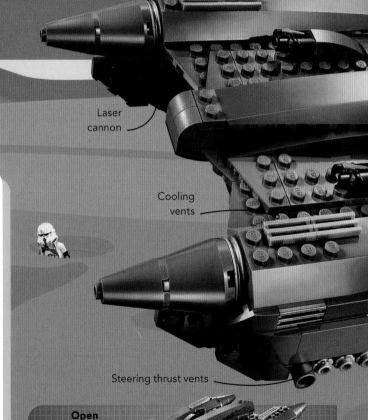

Laser cannon

Cooling vents

Steering thrust vents

As used by ...

General Grievous
Grievous was more machine than man and he could move incredibly fast. But he still couldn't fly without a ship!

Obi-Wan Kenobi
After defeating Grievous on Utapau, Jedi General Obi-Wan Kenobi took the *Soulless One* to escape the planet.

Open cockpit

Main thruster

Rudder used to steer in planetary atmospheres

ALTERNATIVE VIEW

NEED TO KNOW

Model: *Belbullab-22 heavy starfighter*

Length: *6.7 m (22 ft)*

Top speed: *1,100 kph (684 mph)*

Weapons: *Laser cannons*

Made by: *Feethan Ottraw Scalable Assemblies*

TRY BEFORE YOU FLY . . .

Get the Grievous look on the ground with a Separatist combat speeder. Its open-air design gives you room to swing several lightsabers!

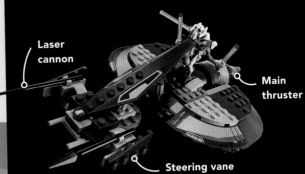

Laser cannon

Main thruster

Steering vane

Performance	Handling
★★★★★	★★★★★
Usability	Overall
★★★★★	★★★★★

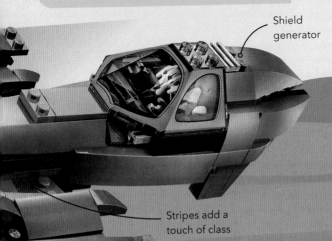

Shield generator

Stripes add a touch of class

SOULLESS ONE

DRIVER'S LICENSE

NAME: General Grievous

ADDRESS: Level 10, Pau City, Utapau (third buzzer)

AGE: Varies (newest parts added last week)

EXPIRES SOON!

FEETHAN OTTRAW SCALABLE ASSEMBLIES

Home of the Belbullab-22 starfighter

"WE PUT THE POW IN UTAPAU!"

Soulless One? Sounds like an old shoe!

JEDI INTERCEPTORS

In the days before the Jedi Order disappeared, they had their own fleet of ships. This included the swift and stylish Eta-2 light interceptor, commonly known as the Jedi interceptor. They became rare after the Empire fell, making this vehicle a collector's dream find.

Excess heat escapes through these open panels

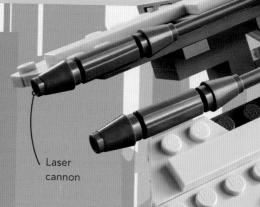

Laser cannon

ALTERNATIVE VIEW

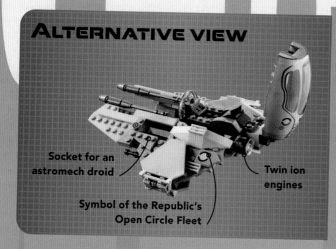

Socket for an astromech droid

Twin ion engines

Symbol of the Republic's Open Circle Fleet

GOING GREEN?

You can't get much greener than Yoda, who flew a version of the Jedi interceptor suited to his size. Like the Jedi Master himself, its environmental footprint was tiny.

Keep an eye on that guy, Artoo!

NO LIGHTSABERS LEFT IN THIS VEHICLE OVERNIGHT

OPTIONAL EXTRAS

Most Jedi pilots use their Force abilities instead of a ship's built-in sensors. Make sure sensors are installed before taking one of these for a spin.

Yellow bodywork found only on Anakin's interceptor

CSA Priority:

[URGENT]

Dear Master Kenobi,
Thank you for your letter about the Coruscant Congestion Charge Payment Order (CCC-PO) made against your Eta-2 Actis-class light interceptor.
Having reviewed your case, I can confirm that we do not need to see your identification and you can go about your business. Move along.
Move along.
Sincerely,
The Coruscant
Skyways Authority

ANAKIN SKYWALKER'S INTERCEPTOR

R2-D2 in astromech socket

NEED TO KNOW

Model: Eta-2 Actis-class light interceptor

Length: 5.5 m (18 ft)

Top speed: 1,500 kph (932 mph)

Weapons: Laser cannons, proton torpedoes

Made by: Kuat Systems Engineering

MISSION LOG

BATTLE OF CORUSCANT

Anakin Skywalker had to crash-land his yellow interceptor on the enemy flagship in this battle—before crash-landing that, too!

MISSION TO MUSTAFAR

When Anakin turned to the dark side, he flew a new, green interceptor to the planet Mustafar on a secret mission for Darth Sidious.

PODRACERS

If you have the need for speed, then a podracer might be the ride for you. They may not look it, but podracers are surprisingly strong and extremely fast! Most famously used on the planet Tatooine, these custom-built craft are made with just one thing in mind—speed!

Sign me up for the pod squad!

Energy binder arc

Adjustable air scoops

👕 WHAT TO WEAR

Podracer cockpits are usually open to the air. You'll need a good pair of goggles to keep the dust (and flying debris from exploding podracers) out of your eyes.

CAUTION!
VEHICLE MAY EXPLODE AT HIGH SPEEDS

NEED TO KNOW

Model: *Anakin Skywalker's Podracer*

Length (engine): *7 m (23 ft)*

Top speed: *947 kph (588 mph)*

Weapons: *None*

Made by: *Custom-built by Anakin himself*

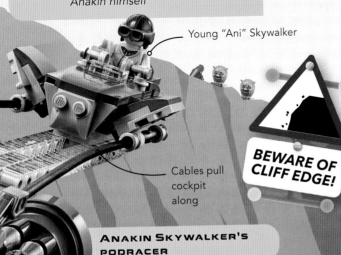

Young "Ani" Skywalker

Cables pull cockpit along

ANAKIN SKYWALKER'S PODRACER

BEWARE OF CLIFF EDGE!

TRY BEFORE YOU FLY . . .

For an exciting but safer way to get around Tatooine, test drive a T-16 skyhopper. It's speedy, reliable, and perfect for outpacing pesky desert womp rats.

Performance
★ ★ ★ ★ ★

Handling
★ ★ ★ ★ ★

Usability
★ ★ ★ ★ ★

Overall
★ ★ ★ ★ ★

Famous Malastarian podracer Sebulba

Circular saw

?? ? OPTIONAL EXTRAS

No two podracers are exactly alike. Champion cheat Sebulba made his with extra-large engines and built-in buzz saws for cutting out the competition.

SKI SPEEDERS

These ships were designed for asteroid slalom races, with a single ski keeping them in contact with the ground at all times. They're just the thing if you want to try the extreme sport. Ski speeders can also be used for exploration and defense, as rebels and Resistance fighters found on the planet Crait.

Resistance fighter **Rose Tico** says: SPRAY YOUR SKI SPEEDER FOR STONE MITES!

Laser cannon pod

SKI SPEEDER

 TRY BEFORE YOU FLY . . .

If you want to sail over sands without kicking up a cloud, try an Arunskin 75D transport skimmer. Be warned—you'll need muscle power to steer.

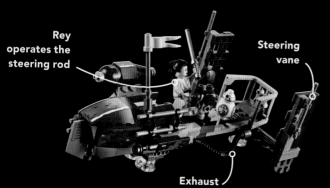

Rey operates the steering rod

Steering vane

Exhaust

Performance
★★★★★

Handling
★★★★★

Usability
★★★★★

Overall
★★★★★

DON'T MISS

The Orleon Belt

It's all downhill from here!

Ski Speeder Slalom Finals!

⚒ MISSION LOG

BATTLE OF CRAIT

Poe, Finn, and Rose Tico used rusty old ski speeders to defend a Resistance base against the First Order on salt-covered Crait.

👕 WHAT TO WEAR

A headset lets you talk to nearby pilots over the roar of your ski speeder engine. It also messes up your hero hairstyle less than a full helmet.

Cooling vents for central engine

PERFECT FOR . . .

Leaving a mark. Ski speeders churn up a trail in the ground behind them.

It's about time I got to test drive something!

Poe flew a ski speeder with the Resistance on the planet Crait

Halofoil mono-ski for stability

📖 NEED TO KNOW

Model: *V-4X-D Ski Speeder*

Width: *11.5 m (38 ft)*

Top speed: *160 kph (99 mph)*

Weapons: *Laser cannons*

Made by: *Roche Machines*

SPEEDER BIKES

There are many different designs of speeder bike, but all put speed ahead of safety. Popular models include the BARC speeders used during the Clone Wars; the 712-AvA used by bounty hunter "the Mandalorian;" and the 74-Z favored by the Empire's biker scouts. Whichever kind you choose, be sure to wear a helmet!

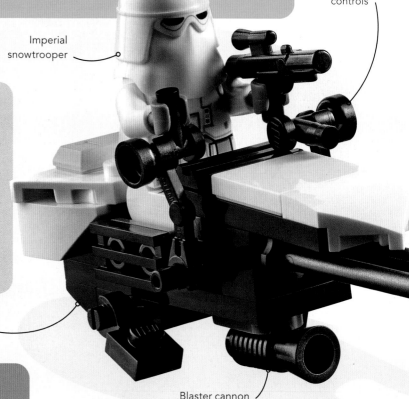

Imperial snowtrooper

Handlebar controls

Blaster cannon

📖 NEED TO KNOW

Model: 74-Z speeder bike

Length: 3.3 m (10 ft)

Top speed: 500 kph (310 mph)

Weapons: Blaster cannon

Made by: Aratech Repulsor Company

Engine directly under seat—toasty!

AS USED BY . . .

Darth Maul
This scary Sith apprentice used a speeder bike called *Bloodfin* to chase his enemies on Tatooine.

Leia Organa
Leia "borrowed" an Imperial 74-Z speeder bike to race through the trees on the Forest Moon of Endor.

You never forget how to ride a speeder bike!

BARC-ING PERMIT

Do **not** tow, ticket, or proton-torpedo this BARC speeder
Biker Advanced Recon Commando on call!

PROS AND CONS
ON A SPEEDER BIKE

👍 Small enough to stash in the back of a compact family starship.

👍 At home anywhere, from the forests of Endor to the icy planet Hoth.

👎 Provides little protection against the elements. Bring your goggles!

👎 Open design makes the vehicle an easy target for attackers.

OWNER'S TIPS

1. Use a tractor beam to secure yourself to the seat.

2. Always keep one foot on the speed-control pedals.

3. Watch out! Speeder bike thieves are always around.

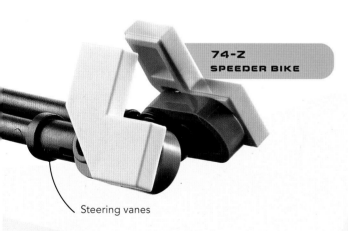

74-Z SPEEDER BIKE

Steering vanes

⚠️ **WARNING** ⚠️
CORONET CITY SHIPYARDS ARE GUARDED BY C-PH PATROL SPEEDER BIKES!

LOOK BOTH WAYS BEFORE CROSSING THE EMPIRE!

Rey
Before she became a Jedi, Rey was a scavenger who built her own speeder bike out of salvaged parts.

31

SOLO WALKERS

Why fly when you can walk? With long metal legs at your disposal, you can stomp around the galaxy without ever breaking a sweat. Large walkers are famously slow, but these solo vehicles are much more fleet of foot. Some can even leap their way over long distances.

TRY BEFORE YOU FLY . . .

If you really want to walk with your head held high, seek out one of the blue AT-RTs used by the elite 501st Clone Battalion.

501st clone trooper

Blue bodywork matches trooper's armor

Performance
★★★★★

Handling
★★★★★

Usability
★★★★★

Overall
★★★★★

?? ? OPTIONAL EXTRAS

Some AT-RTs have flamethrowers instead of blaster cannons. Others use noise-reduction technology to sound like they are walking on tiptoes.

WATCH YOUR STEP!

WOOKIEES CROSSING

RRRRGGGGH!

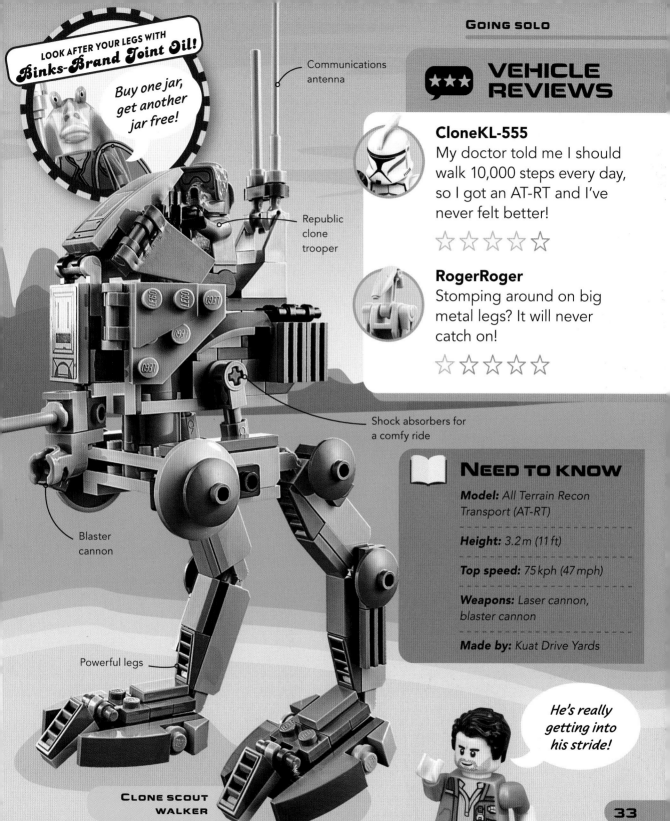

Communications antenna

Republic clone trooper

★★★ VEHICLE REVIEWS

CloneKL-555
My doctor told me I should walk 10,000 steps every day, so I got an AT-RT and I've never felt better!

★★★★☆

RogerRoger
Stomping around on big metal legs? It will never catch on!

☆☆☆☆☆

Shock absorbers for a comfy ride

Blaster cannon

Powerful legs

CLONE SCOUT WALKER

📖 NEED TO KNOW

Model: *All Terrain Recon Transport (AT-RT)*

Height: *3.2 m (11 ft)*

Top speed: *75 kph (47 mph)*

Weapons: *Laser cannon, blaster cannon*

Made by: *Kuat Drive Yards*

He's really getting into his stride!

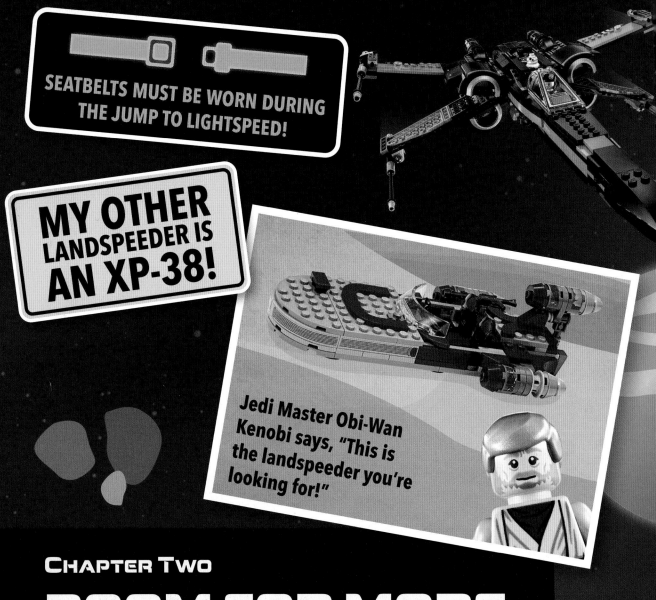

SEATBELTS MUST BE WORN DURING THE JUMP TO LIGHTSPEED!

MY OTHER LANDSPEEDER IS AN XP-38!

Jedi Master Obi-Wan Kenobi says, "This is the landspeeder you're looking for!"

CHAPTER TWO

ROOM FOR MORE

Bring your friends along for the ride in these small-to-medium modes of transportation. Spanning everything from two-person snowspeeders to family-size shuttles, this selection has the right fit for everyone—and their luggage, too!

For sale:

UT-60D U-wing starfighter/ support craft

U looking for a spacious family vehicle? U need this pre-loved U-wing! Slightly scratched (okay, more than slightly) following the Battle of Scarif. U need more details? Call Blue Squadron.

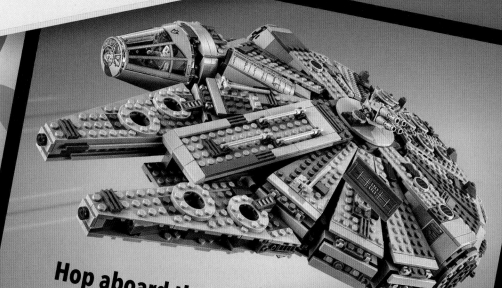

Hop aboard the Millennium Falcon for a ride in the fastest ship in the galaxy!

LANDSPEEDERS

Landspeeders are bigger than speeder bikes but small enough to use in busy towns and cities. They can't fly high, hovering just above the ground. Still, these easy-to-drive vehicles are popular for making short journeys in a jiffy.

SPEEDER-NEEDER MONTHLY

Now incorporating Repulsorcraft Review

This issue: Test-driving the new M-68 M-barrassing or Gr-8?

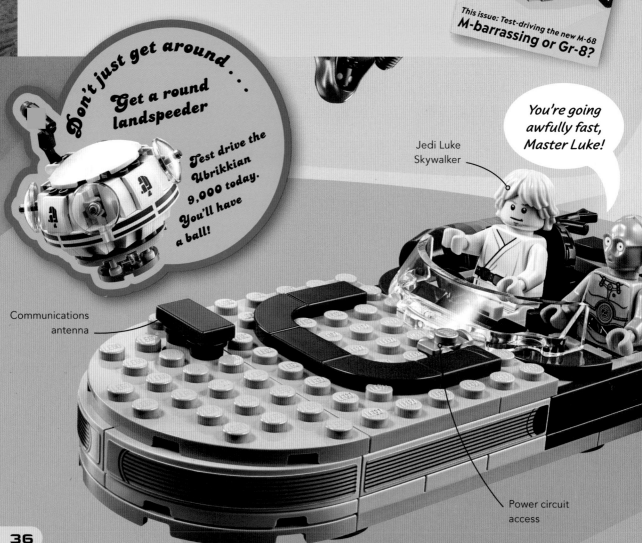

Don't just get around . . .
Get a round landspeeder

Test drive the Ubrikkian 9,000 today. You'll have a ball!

Jedi Luke Skywalker

You're going awfully fast, Master Luke!

Communications antenna

Power circuit access

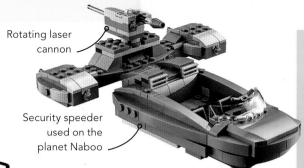

Rotating laser cannon

Security speeder used on the planet Naboo

 ## OPTIONAL EXTRAS

Landspeeders are often upgraded with blaster cannons. If you get one with a top-mounted cannon, remember to duck before you fire!

AS USED BY . . .

Luke Skywalker
This farm boy began his journey to becoming a Jedi when he set out in his speeder to find Obi-Wan Kenobi.

Han Solo
Young Han used a sporty M-68 landspeeder to escape from the White Worms crime gang on Corellia.

Moloch
This White Worm gangster chased Han in a heavy-duty A-A4B landspeeder, also known as a truckspeeder.

 ## NEED TO KNOW

Model: *X-34 Landspeeder*

Length: *3.4 m (11 ft)*

Top speed: *250 kph (155 mph)*

Weapons: *None*

Made by: *SoroSuub Corporation*

LUKE SKYWALKER'S LANDSPEEDER

Repulsor technology keeps the speeder off the ground

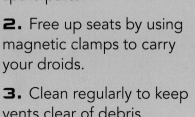 ## OWNER'S TIPS

1. Stock up on high quality spare parts.

2. Free up seats by using magnetic clamps to carry your droids.

3. Clean regularly to keep vents clear of debris.

With one of these you'll be floating on air!

SNOWSPEEDERS

On the icy world of Hoth, rebel engineers adapted airspeeders into snowspeeders that could withstand extreme winter weather. If you need to fly around in sub-zero temperatures, then this zippy vehicle might be just the thing for you. Why not try one out before you get cold feet?

DANGER! TRIPPING HAZARD

Magnetic grapple intended for towing cargo

Brake flaps lift for slowing and stopping

TRY BEFORE YOU FLY . . .

If you want to chill with a bigger crew, check out the First Order's take on the snowspeeder. It might not be stylish, but it's spacious!

Fold-down rear seats

Standing room

Fuel tank access

Performance
★★★★★

Handling
★★★★★

Usability
★★★★★

Overall
★★★★★

 NEED TO KNOW

Model: Modified T-47 Airspeeder

Length: 5.3 m (17 ft)

Top speed: 1,100 kph (684 mph)

Weapons: Laser cannons, grapple gun

Made by: Incom Corporation

✖ MISSION LOG

BATTLE OF HOTH

Snowspeeders helped the rebels defend themselves against the Empire during the attack on Hoth.

ATTENTION SNOWSPEEDER PILOTS!
BRUSH OFF **BEAST** ATTACKS
with

WAMPA WIPERS!

That tickles!

From the makers of Sarlacc Scarers and Zillo Beast Zappers

Cockpit has room for a pilot and rear gunner

SNOWSPEEDER

Sandspeeder

This isn't what Tatooine looked like in the brochure...

OPTIONAL EXTRAS

If you like the look of the snowspeeder but don't like the cold, you're in luck! It can be adapted for desert conditions as the T-47 sandspeeder.

Snow doubt about it, that's cool!

AS USED BY...

Zev Senesca
When Luke Skywalker and Han Solo went missing on Hoth, rebel Zev used his snowspeeder to find them.

Wedge Antilles
This pilot and his gunner, Wes Janson, used the speeder's cable to trip an Imperial AT-AT on Hoth.

U-WING STARFIGHTERS

Unlike other starfighters, the U-wing also serves as a troop transport. There is room for eight passengers who can leap into combat from sliding doors. This is the starfighter to choose if you want a roomy vehicle to carry troops, a spacious family vehicle, or both.

Hey U!
U need U-wing retuning?
We tune U-wings
WHILE-U-WAIT!
NO IOUs!
Next U-turn

Laser cannon

Long swing-wing foils face forward in normal flight

NEED TO KNOW

Model: *UT-60D U-wing starfighter/ support craft*

Length: *25 m (82 ft)*

Top speed: *950 kph (590 mph)*

Weapons: *Laser cannons, ion blaster*

Made by: *Incom Corporation*

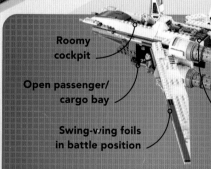

Roomy cockpit

Open passenger/ cargo bay

Fusion chamber cooling vents

Swing-wing foils in battle position

ALTERNATIVE VIEW

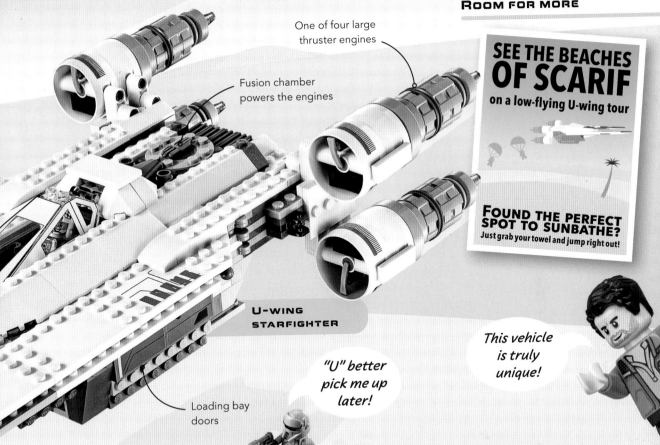

One of four large
thruster engines

Fusion chamber
powers the engines

**SEE THE BEACHES
OF SCARIF**
on a low-flying U-wing tour

**FOUND THE PERFECT
SPOT TO SUNBATHE?**
Just grab your towel and jump right out!

U-WING
STARFIGHTER

*This vehicle
is truly
unique!*

*"U" better
pick me up
later!*

Loading bay
doors

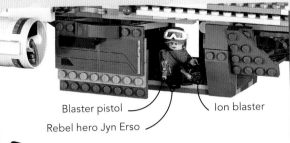

Blaster pistol

Rebel hero Jyn Erso

Ion blaster

 OPTIONAL EXTRAS

The rebels added hand-
operated weapons to the
underside of their U-wings,
for use by passengers hanging
out of the side doors.

⚒ MISSION LOG

OPERATION FRACTURE

Rebel spy Cassian Andor
flew a U-wing to find out
more about a new Imperial
superweapon—the infamous
Death Star!

BATTLE OF SCARIF

U-wings formed part of the
fleet that helped the "Rogue
One" rebels steal the Death
Star plans from under the
Empire's noses.

MANDALORIAN STARFIGHTERS

STOP

In the name of Mandalore!

Most Mandalorians are not keen on other species using their technology. If you don't mind being challenged to prove your worthiness every time you meet someone from Mandalore, this sleek starfighter could be the ship for you.

DRIVER'S LICENSE

NAME:
Bo-Katan Kryze

ADDRESS:
Mandalore

EYE COLOR:
Green

HAIR COLOR:
Red

HEIGHT:
1.8 m
(5 ft 11 in)

ID PHOTO REJECTED

??? OPTIONAL EXTRAS

Mandalorian starfighters come in a range of sizes. If your ship is big enough, you can get extra-large laser cannons at the front and back.

BO-KATAN KRYZE'S MANDALORIAN STARFIGHTER

AS USED BY . . .

Pre Vizsla
This ruler of Mandalore commanded a fleet of *Kom'rk*-class fighters, the Gauntlet starfighters.

Bo-Katan Kryze
The Mando warrior flew a Gauntlet fighter on a mission to rescue the Child, Grogu.

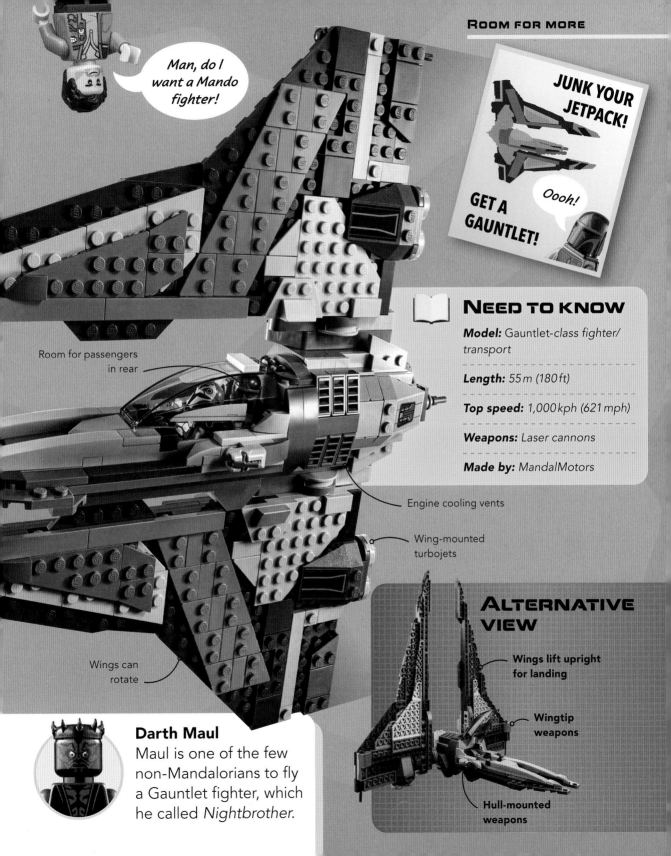

Man, do I want a Mando fighter!

JUNK YOUR JETPACK!

GET A GAUNTLET!

Oooh!

NEED TO KNOW

Model: *Gauntlet-class* fighter/transport

Length: 55 m (180 ft)

Top speed: 1,000 kph (621 mph)

Weapons: Laser cannons

Made by: MandalMotors

Room for passengers in rear

Engine cooling vents

Wing-mounted turbojets

Wings can rotate

ALTERNATIVE VIEW

Wings lift upright for landing

Wingtip weapons

Hull-mounted weapons

Darth Maul
Maul is one of the few non-Mandalorians to fly a Gauntlet fighter, which he called *Nightbrother*.

RESISTANCE BOMBERS

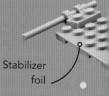

The long, lower part of this unusual-looking ship is meant to be packed full of proton bombs. But peace-loving pilots may find it also comes in handy when they have a lot of shopping. There's plenty of room for friends as well, so no one needs to be dropped!

Stabilizer foil

?? ? OPTIONAL EXTRAS

The bomb bays in StarFortress bombers can be converted to hold liquids. They can be used as fuel tankers or even flying fire engines.

PERFECT FOR . . .

Making large deliveries to enemy bases, whether they want them or not!

YOU'LL MAKE A GREATER CRATER in a **StarFortress** SF-17!

Visit your nearest Slayn & Korpil dealer today!

AS USED BY . . .

Finch Dallow
Fearless Finch faced the First Order as pilot of the Resistance bomber *Cobalt Hammer* during the Battle of D'Qar.

Paige Tico
While Finch flew the *Cobalt Hammer*, Paige prepped the proton bombs and pressed the buttons to launch them.

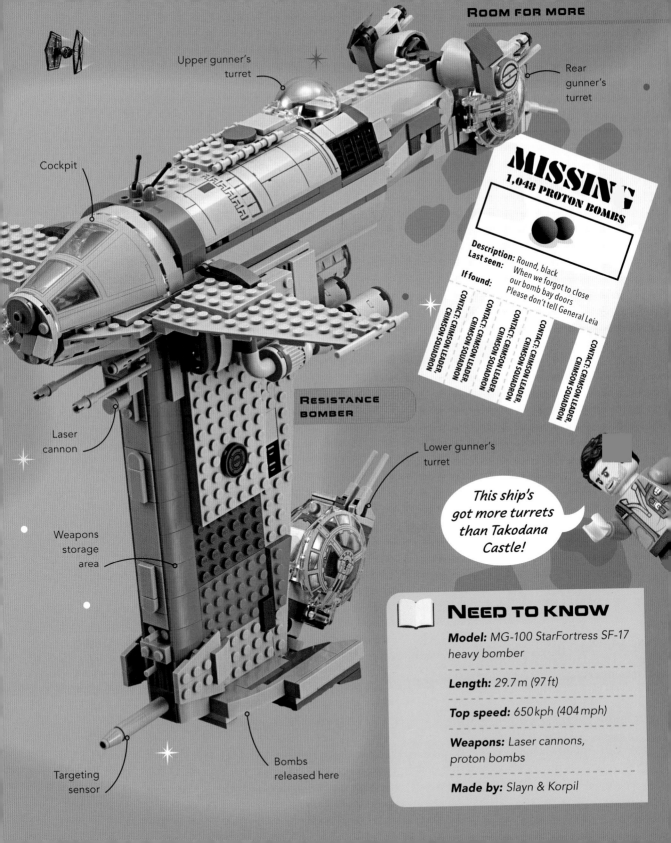

Upper gunner's turret

Rear gunner's turret

Cockpit

Laser cannon

Weapons storage area

Targeting sensor

Bombs released here

Lower gunner's turret

RESISTANCE BOMBER

MISSING
1,048 PROTON BOMBS

Description: Round, black
Last seen: When we forgot to close our bomb bay doors
If found: Please don't tell General Leia

CONTACT: CRIMSON LEADER, CRIMSON SQUADRON
CONTACT: CRIMSON LEADER, CRIMSON SQUADRON
CONTACT: CRIMSON LEADER, CRIMSON SQUADRON
CONTACT: CRIMSON LEADER, CRIMSON SQUADRON
CONTACT: CRIMSON LEADER, CRIMSON SQUADRON
CONTACT: CRIMSON LEADER, CRIMSON SQUADRON

This ship's got more turrets than Takodana Castle!

NEED TO KNOW

Model: MG-100 StarFortress SF-17 heavy bomber

Length: 29.7 m (97 ft)

Top speed: 650 kph (404 mph)

Weapons: Laser cannons, proton bombs

Made by: Slayn & Korpil

IMPERIAL SHUTTLES

Imperial ships aren't famed for their looks, but the design favored by the Emperor is in a class of its own. *Lambda*-class shuttles are sleek and stylish with their elegant folding wings. This is the shuttle you want to arrive in when you go to a glitzy party.

EMPIRE TODAY
IN-FLIGHT MAGAZINE

INSIDE: TALKIN' TARKIN
Get the Imperial look
10 things you never knew about superweapons

VEHICLE REVIEWS

DarkLord66
It's great, but I ordered a black one.

☆☆☆☆☆

TK_9714
Would be better if there were windows . . . or if I was allowed to sit in the front.

☆☆☆☆☆

ALTERNATIVE VIEW

Wings in landing mode

Rear laser cannons

Ion engines

Lower stabilizer wings fold up for landing

AS USED BY . . .

Emperor Palpatine
Sith Lords like to make a grand entrance. No one could miss the arrival of the Emperor's shiny shuttle.

Governor Tarkin
The man in charge of the first Death Star was one of many Imperial officers to fly in a *Lambda*-class shuttle.

Upper stabilizer wing

Windowless passenger area

Laser cannons

Blaster cannons

LAMBDA-CLASS IMPERIAL SHUTTLE

📖 NEED TO KNOW

Model: Lambda-class T-4a shuttle

Length: 20 m (66 ft)

Top speed: 850 kph (528 mph)

Weapons: Laser cannons, blaster cannons

Made by: Sienar Fleet Systems

PILOTS: KNOW YOUR CLEARANCE CODES!

Imperial command stations will no longer drop shields for:

> Older clearance codes

> Clearance codes you borrowed from someone else

> Excuses about how a womp rat ate your clearance codes

> Cookies

🕴 TRY BEFORE YOU FLY . . .

The *Sentinel*-class shuttle offers extra space for additional troop transport. The ship can also carry heavy weapons.

Folding wings

Landing ski

Passenger ramp

Performance
★★★★★

Handling
★★★★★

Usability
★★★★★

Overall
★★★★★

Han Solo
Han used the Imperial shuttle to help the rebels get close to the second Death Star's key defenses.

ATTACK SHUTTLES

Omicron-class attack shuttles were used by the Galactic Republic during the Clone Wars, and by "Bad Batch" Clone Force 99 in the Imperial era. These mean, muscular ships don't look as grand as Imperial shuttles, but they certainly live up to their name.

HERE COMES THE MARAUDER CLONE FORCE 99

PROS AND CONS

IN AN *OMICRON*-CLASS ATTACK SHUTTLE

👍 All the benefits of a starfighter and a shuttle in one ship.

👍 Cool to fly the same kind of ship as the elite Clone Force 99.

👎 No element of surprise when you attack in an attack shuttle!

👎 Dangerous to risk being mistaken for Clone Force 99!

AS USED BY . . .

Hunter
This clone commando led Clone Force 99 on board the *Marauder*, a modified *Omicron*-class shuttle.

Tech
The brains of Clone Force 99 once got the *Marauder* captured by the Empire as part of a cunning plan!

NEED TO KNOW

Model: Omicron-class attack shuttle

Length: 30.3 m (99 ft)

Top speed: 750 kph (466 mph)

Weapons: Laser cannons

Made by: Cygnus Spaceworks

Formation lights switch on and off for stealth missions

THE MARAUDER

Tune in to **PILOT RADIO** for tips on tuning up your vehicle

This week join the "Bad Batch" for 99 ways to keep it shipshape.

Heavily armored cockpit

Reinforced view ports

Laser cannons

SHUTTLE PARKING ONLY!

▶ Please turn off engines and fold up wings

▶ Passenger shuttles left at owner's risk

▶ Attack shuttles left at everyone else's risk

This ship's more shark than shuttle!

Wrecker
Another member of Clone Force 99, Wrecker made many repairs and upgrades to the *Marauder*.

Folding stabilizer wings

KYLO REN'S SHUTTLE

When the First Order looked back on the Empire's shuttles, they decided they were good, but they just weren't intimidating enough! Why not try out a bat-shaped *Upsilon*-class shuttle like Kylo Ren's? It has plenty of room for passengers . . . or prisoners.

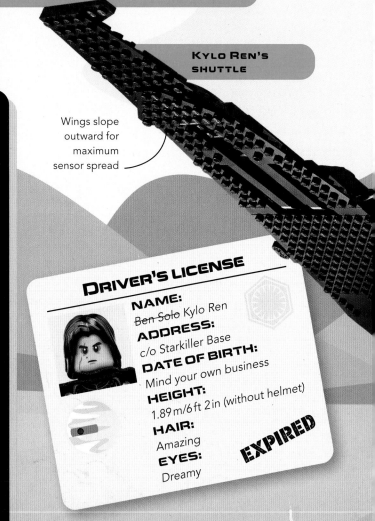

KYLO REN'S SHUTTLE

Wings slope outward for maximum sensor spread

TRY BEFORE YOU FLY . . .

For a dark side ride on the smaller side, try the experimental TIE silencer. It has the same Sith attitude without the passenger seats.

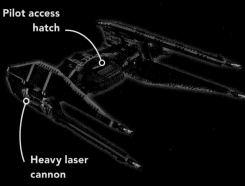

Pilot access hatch

Heavy laser cannon

Performance
★★★★★

Handling
★★★★★

Usability
★★★★★

Overall
★★★★★

DRIVER'S LICENSE

NAME:
~~Ben Solo~~ Kylo Ren

ADDRESS:
c/o Starkiller Base

DATE OF BIRTH:
Mind your own business

HEIGHT:
1.89 m/6 ft 2 in (without helmet)

HAIR:
Amazing

EYES:
Dreamy

EXPIRED

Wings packed with sensors and stealth tech

Ion engines

Heavy laser cannon

Landing lights

NEED TO KNOW

Model: Upsilon-*class shuttle*

Length: *19 m (63 ft)*

Top speed: *950 kph (590 mph)*

Weapons: *Heavy laser cannons*

Made by: *Sienar-Jaemus Fleet Systems*

VEHICLE REVIEWS

VaderWasMyGrampa
This is obviously the best-ever shuttle and the pilot is the best-ever pilot. Kylo Ren is SO COOL and should definitely rule the galaxy.

☆☆☆☆☆

General_Hux
You know you've posted this from your main account, right?

MISSION LOG

ATTACK ON TAKODANA
Kylo Ren captured Rey in this First Order strike, taking her to Starkiller Base in his *Upsilon*-class shuttle.

BATTLE OF CRAIT
Ren took his command shuttle into the heart of this battle hoping to cross laser swords with Luke Skywalker.

Nobody tell Ren that I like his ship!

BOBA FETT'S STARSHIP

Before this ship was Boba Fett's, it belonged to Boba's father, Jango, who was also a bounty hunter. If you want to fly it, you'll need to get to grips with all the hidden upgrades the Fetts have made over the years . . . and be sure to get Boba's permission first!

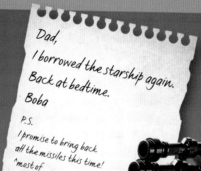

Dad,
I borrowed the starship again.
Back at bedtime.
Boba

P.S.
I promise to bring back
^most of all the missiles this time!

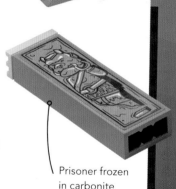

I hope he's not looking for me!

VEHICLE REVIEWS

TheWanNOnlyKenobi
I didn't think flying could get any worse until I tried to outfly this starship!

☆☆☆☆☆

BountyHunter4Hire
This is really *not* a fast ship. And it definitely doesn't have lots of hidden weapons. If you see it coming, relax. You've got nothing to worry about!

☆☆☆☆☆

Rotating blaster cannon

??? OPTIONAL EXTRAS

Boba's ship is full of hidden weapons, sensors, and shields. He even fitted it with space for carbonite-frozen prisoners.

Prisoner frozen in carbonite

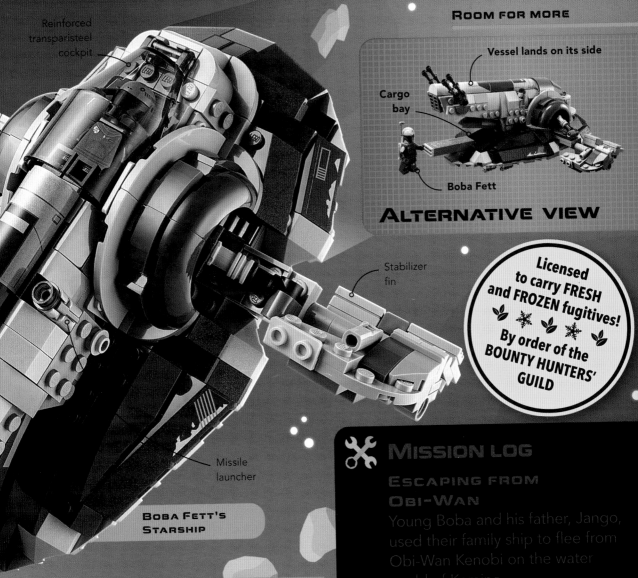

Reinforced transparisteel cockpit

Vessel lands on its side

Cargo bay

Boba Fett

ALTERNATIVE VIEW

Stabilizer fin

Licensed to carry FRESH and FROZEN fugitives!

✿ ❄ ✿

By order of the BOUNTY HUNTERS' GUILD

Missile launcher

BOBA FETT'S STARSHIP

🔧 MISSION LOG

ESCAPING FROM OBI-WAN
Young Boba and his father, Jango, used their family ship to flee from Obi-Wan Kenobi on the water world of Kamino.

HUNTING FOR HAN
When Darth Vader used bounty hunters to find Han Solo, Boba Fett's starship won the race to track him down.

GOING AFTER GROGU
Boba Fett and his starship helped the Mandalorian get to Grogu when he was kidnapped.

📖 NEED TO KNOW

Model: *Modified Firespray-31-class patrol and attack craft*

Length: *21.5 m (71 ft)*

Top speed: *1,000 kph (621 mph)*

Weapons: *Laser cannons, blaster cannons, ion cannon, proton torpedoes, concussion missiles, seismic charges*

Made by: *Kuat Systems Engineering*

RAZOR CREST

This classic ship was built before the Empire was founded. The *Razor Crest* eventually became the modified motor home of the bounty hunter Din Djarin, known as the Mandalorian, and the Child, Grogu. It may not be much to look at, but the *Razor Crest* is both roomy and functional.

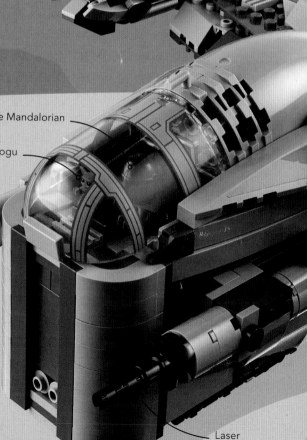

CHILD ON BOARD!

The Mandalorian

Grogu

Laser cannon

📖 NEED TO KNOW

Model: *ST-70 M-111 Razor Crest assault gunship*

Length: *25 m (80 ft)*

Top speed: *800 kph (497 mph)*

Weapons: *Laser cannons*

Made by: *Belsmuth Consolidations Ltd.*

RAZOR CREST LOGBOOK

Day 1:	Attacked
Day 2:	Attacked
Day 3:	Repairs
Day 4:	Attacked; attacked; repairs; attacked again
Day 6:	Crashed; sank; repairs; attacked
Day 7:	Blew up

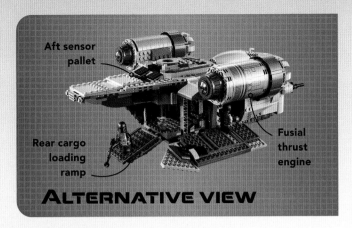

Aft sensor pallet

Rear cargo loading ramp

Fusial thrust engine

ALTERNATIVE VIEW

VEHICLE REVIEWS

Mando_Man
I would recommend this ship for long journeys, especially if you're traveling with children.

☆☆☆☆☆

Oversize engine

RAZOR CREST

OPTIONAL EXTRAS

Picking up a second-hand ship means you can customize it. Going one better than fellow bounty hunter Boba Fett, the Mandalorian had his own carbonite freezing chamber built into the *Razor Crest*.

GOING GREEN?

By keeping the Razor Crest in service for so many years, the Mandalorian certainly did his bit for reducing galactic waste!

MILLENNIUM FALCON

If you want your own ship, you might have ruled out owning something as famous as the *Millennium Falcon*. But think again, because Rey found the *Falcon* in a Jakku junkyard. You could soon be behind the controls of the fastest ship in the skies!

FASTEST... OF JUNK IN THE GALAXY!

NEED TO KNOW

Model: Modified YT-1300f light freighter

Length: 34.5 m (113 ft)

Top speed: 1,050 kph (652 mph)

Weapons: Laser cannons, concussion missiles, blaster cannon, tractor beam projectors

Made by: Corellian Engineering Corporation

Finn in the copilot's seat

Rey at the controls

Maintenance hatch

AS USED BY . . .

Lando Calrissian
Lando turned the *Falcon* from a freighter into a speedy sports craft before Han Solo won it from him in a card game.

Han Solo
Han's adventures did a lot of damage to the ship. The savvy smuggler also upgraded the weapons and engines.

WELCOME TO HYPERSPACE STAY IN LANE

Quad laser cannon

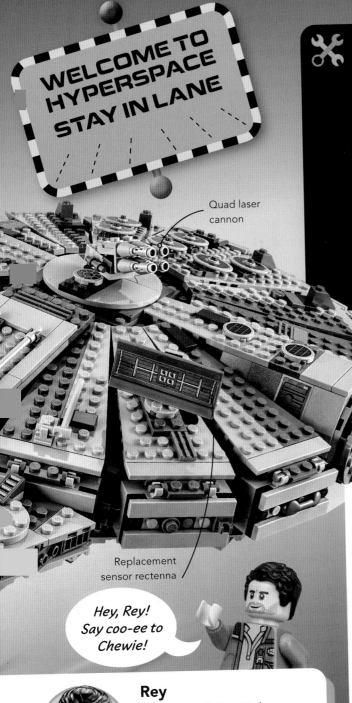

MILLENNIUM FALCON

Docking port

Replacement sensor rectenna

Hey, Rey! Say coo-ee to Chewie!

Rey
Rey found the *Falcon* by chance. Han Solo and his copilot Chewbacca soon saw that she was born to fly it.

🔧 MISSION LOG

BATTLE OF YAVIN
Han and Chewie were late to this battle, but the *Falcon* arrived just in time to send Darth Vader's ship into a spin.

BATTLE OF ENDOR
Lando flew the *Falcon* inside the second Death Star, blowing it to bits with a daring attack on its power core.

LOOKING FOR LUKE
Rey and Chewbacca flew the *Falcon* to the planet Ahch-To, where they found the long-lost Jedi Luke Skywalker.

Single laser cannon

Sensor dish

Escape pod

Young Han on a mission for Lando

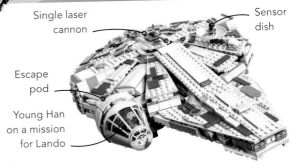

?? **OPTIONAL EXTRAS**

Back when it was a shiny racing ship, Lando had the *Falcon* fitted with a two-person escape pod between its cargo-pushing prongs.

JAWA JIVE
50 desert driving anthems to shake your sandcrawler!

Featuring:
The Max Rebo Band – Sy Snootles – Figrin D'an and many more!

AT-AT—when you want to walk, but not with your own feet.

CHAPTER THREE

EXTRA LEG ROOM

They may not be the biggest craft in the galaxy, but these mega machines are far more spacious than most. From towering AT-ATs to sprawling sandcrawlers, you can seat dozens in these roomy runarounds, especially if the passengers are Jawas.

DON'T WALK

WALK

LOW-ALTITUDE ASSAULT CRAFT LANDING ZONE
LOOK LEFT, LOOK RIGHT, LOOK UP!

See the **GALAXY** *in your* **LAAT**

REPUBLIC GUNSHIPS

Designed to carry clones between orbiting ships and ground battles, low-altitude assault transports (LAATs) are built for short trips. Up to 30 passengers can fit inside, but there are wide-open sides instead of walls and no seats. So be sure to hold on tight!

Mass-driver missile launchers

 ## NEED TO KNOW

Model: *Low-Altitude Assault Transport/infantry (LAAT/i)*

Length: *17.4 m (57 ft)*

Top speed: *620 kph (385 mph)*

Weapons: *Laser cannons, mass-driver missiles, air-to-air rockets*

Made by: *Rothana Heavy Engineering*

Twin cockpits for pilot and copilot

Laser cannons

Side-mounted laser turret can swing back into the passenger bay

PERFECT FOR . . .
People who like fresh air and enclosed spaces—all at the same time!

I've heard of taking a side, but this is ridiculous!

MISSION LOG

BATTLE OF GEONOSIS
The Clone Wars began with this battle, as LAATs launched thousands of clone troopers into combat against a vast droid army.

BATTLE OF UTAPAU
A fleet of LAATs came to the aid of Jedi Master Obi-Wan Kenobi when he confronted General Grievous in his lair.

Welcome aboard this Galactic Republic LAAT/i service to: *Utapau*

✓ Please HOLD THE HANDRAILS, MIND THE GAPS, and TAKE ALL BLASTERS WITH YOU WHEN YOU LEAVE.

✕ Please do not PLAY LOUD MUSIC, EAT SMELLY FOOD, or TOUCH THE MISSILES.

You must have SPECIAL PERMISSION to SIT INSIDE THE LASER TURRETS.

Enjoy your ride!

FOR YOUR SAFETY

Please keep arms, legs, and lightsabers inside the vehicle AT ALL TIMES.

REPUBLIC GUNSHIP

Wing-mounted laser turret

Passenger bay can also be used for cargo

? ? ? OPTIONAL EXTRAS

Get artwork painted on your LAAT, just like the troopers did during the Clone Wars. Your ship will be recognizable and unique!

🌿 GOING GREEN?

Ride sharing is always a green choice. LAATs would make for great group transport on any planet!

AT-ATs

All Terrain Armored Transports are a feat of engineering. One AT-AT can march more than 40 Imperial troopers into battle, with room for speeder bikes in the back. They also offer great views of wherever you're going, and leave heavy footprints to show where you've been.

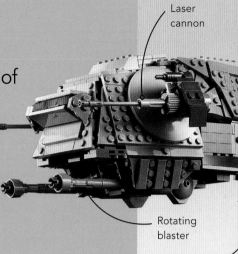

Laser cannon

Rotating blaster

Hip joint

F ROS AND CONS *IN AN AT-AT*

 Very slow compared to a speeder.

👍 Great if you don't like flying.

 Not so great if you don't like heights.

👍 Perfect if you always wanted a pony!*

*A really, really big pony!

📖 NEED TO KNOW

Model: *All Terrain Armored Transport (AT-AT)*

- - - - - - - - - - - - - -
Height: *22.2 m (73 ft)*

- - - - - - - - - - - - - -
Top speed: *60 kph (37 mph)*

- - - - - - - - - - - - - -
Weapons: *Laser cannons, blasters*

- - - - - - - - - - - - - -
Made by: *Kuat Drive Yards*

IMPERIAL AT-AT

✖ MISSION LOG

BATTLE OF HOTH
AT-ATs trekked through ice and snow on frozen Hoth, only to be tripped up by the tow-ropes of rebel snowspeeders.

BATTLE OF JAKKU
Years after an AT-AT fell in this desert battle, Rey used its shell as a base for her scavenging missions.

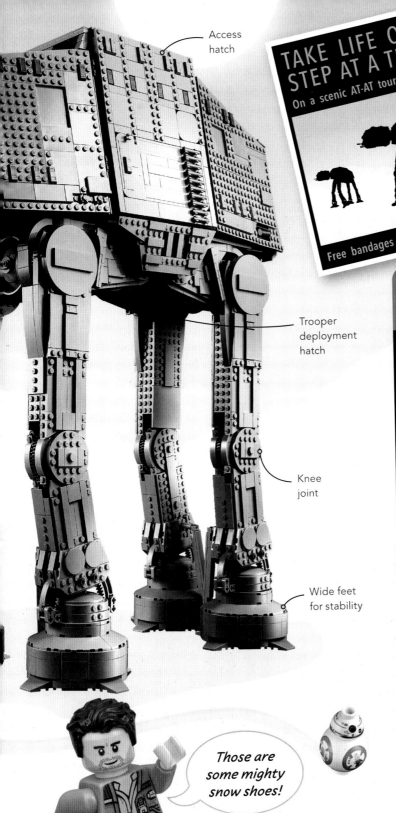

Access hatch

Trooper deployment hatch

Knee joint

Wide feet for stability

TAKE LIFE ONE STEP AT A TIME
On a scenic AT-AT tour of Hoth

Free bandages with every trip!

DON'T AT-AT ME!

Country walkers against Imperial walkers

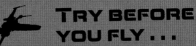

TRY BEFORE YOU FLY . . .

The First Order Heavy Assault Walker is even more animal-like than an AT-AT. It prowls on two back feet and two front "knuckles" like a giant gorilla.

MegaCaliber Six turbolaser cannon

Laser cannon

Gorilla-like "arms"

Performance
★★★★★

Handling
★★★★★

Usability
★★★★★

Overall
★★★★★

Those are some mighty snow shoes!

AT-TEs

These six-legged stompers saw plenty of action in the Clone Wars. Afterward, clone Captain Rex turned one into a roving retirement home for himself and two clone chums. If you're looking for a mobile home, why not follow in the footsteps of Rex and modify your own AT-TE?

Cockpit

 Owner's tips

1. For an extra burst of speed, be sure to clear out all unnecessary cargo.

2. Never operate the mass driver cannon while drowsy.

3. Remember to scrub behind the knees on a regular basis.*

*Even if you don't have an AT-TE

Commander Wolffe on the added observation platform

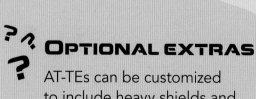

Galactic Retirement Guide
New ideas for aging adventurers!

The AT-TE includes . . .
• Comfortable bunks
• Fully fitted kitchen
• Fishing line to enjoy angling on the go!

 Optional extras

AT-TEs can be customized to include heavy shields and special equipment to let them climb up cliffs and even walk upside down!

Captain Rex operating the mass driver cannon

What a way to make a live-in!

Custom landing pad

Custom cargo lift

REX'S AT-TE

TRAVEL BY AT-TE

More than a million clone troopers can't be wrong!

We love it!

AS USED BY . . .

Captain Rex
This clone captain just wanted a quiet life when he set up his AT-TE home on the distant desert world of Seelos.

Commander Gregor
Rex's best retirement buddy spent his days using their aging AT-TE as a base for hunting giant joopa worms!

Commander Wolffe
After leaving their live-in AT-TE, Wolffe and Gregor found a new home—inside an abandoned Imperial AT-AT!

NEED TO KNOW

Model: Modified All-Terrain Tactical Enforcer (AT-TE)

Length: 22.2 m (73 ft)

Top speed: 45 kph (28 mph)

Weapons: Laser cannons, mass driver cannon

Made by: Rothana Heavy Engineering

SANDCRAWLERS

In a dusty desert, reliability beats speed every time! Slow and steady sandcrawlers are custom-built for desert driving, and their engines won't get clogged with sand like fast-flying skiffs and speeders. They're also big enough to carry plenty of spare parts and even your own Jawa repair crew.

Control room windows

VEHICLE REVIEWS

Says_Threepio
You wouldn't catch me in a sandcrawler. Only the most foolish droid would flag one down for a ride!

☆☆☆☆☆

Artoo_Reviews
Bleepity-boop-bloop boop!

Says_Threepio
Well that's not how I remember it!

GOING GREEN?

Most sandcrawlers have been around for hundreds of years with no signs of wearing out. That makes them an eco-friendly choice.

Dark, cave-like interior

You must be **THIS TALL** to ride the sandcrawler

Cargo sled

Boarding ramp

NEED TO KNOW

Model: *Sandcrawler*

Length: *37 m (121 ft)*

Top speed: *30 kph (19 mph)*

Weapons: *None*

Made by: *Corellia Mining Corporation*

JAWA
SANDCRAWLER

MISSION LOG

MINING MACHINES

Sandcrawlers were originally used by mining companies. When they abandoned their machines, the local Jawas moved in.

MOVING MARKETS

Most Jawas live in modified sandcrawlers. They fill the vehicles with scrap and then trade it with other desert dwellers.

Loading hatch

TRACKS OF TATOOINE

A SPOTTER'S GUIDE

Bantha

Dewback

Sandcrawler

Lost droids

Speeder

Continuous tracks

Jawa trader

Droid for sale

Even longer than the Imperial Star Destroyer!

Resurgent-class Star Destroyer

CARPOOL SPACE LANE
For vehicles with 10,000 passengers or more

THIS STAR DESTROYER IS A SNOKE-FREE ZONE

BY ORDER OF SUPREME LEADER KYLO REN

CHAPTER FOUR

ALL ABOARD

When size matters more than where you're going to park, these vast vessels are just the ticket. The smallest vehicles in this chapter can easily carry hundreds, while the supersize Death Star was home to hundreds of thousands! There's room for everyone in these craft.

– DEATH STAR II –

A SHINING STAR ON THE DARK SIDE

TRAVEL TOGETHER ON BOARD A HAVw A6 JUGGERNAUT

STAR WARS
DEATH STAR
Owner's Workshop Manual

CLONE TURBO TANKS

Flying, hovering, and walking on huge metal legs all have their place in the galaxy, but sometimes you can't beat a set of big wheels. These "monster trucks" are ideal for off-road drivers looking to get away from it all, especially if they're traveling with hundreds of friends.

Short range laser cannons

CLONE TURBO TANK

Heavy laser cannon

Rear cockpit windows

That clone lookout is a real high roller!

Five wheels on either side

Clone commander in camouflage gear

📖 NEED TO KNOW

Model: HAVw A6 Juggernaut

Length: 50 m (162 ft)

Top speed: 160 kph (99 mph)

Weapons: Laser cannons, blaster cannons, missile launchers

Made by: Kuat Drive Yards

Extendable lookout post

Missile launcher

Front cockpit windows

Blaster cannon

PROS AND CONS
IN A CLONE TURBO TANK

👍 Wheels spread weight better than walker legs, so less chance of sinking.

👎 All 10 wheels are huge, so there's no room to travel with a spare one.

👍 Cockpits at both ends means no need to turn to reverse direction.

👎 Cockpits at both ends can cause arguments about who's at the front.

Antennae can be retracted

Legs fold away for storage

AT-RT walker

⁇ OPTIONAL EXTRAS

Turbo tanks allow for lots of different internal layouts. The most popular design includes room for at least one AT-RT walker.

TANTIVE IV

The *Tantive IV* is fit for diplomats, dignitaries, and even princesses. This classic corvette isn't just for glad-handing and gourmet dinners, however. Combined with six turbolaser turrets and 11 ion engines, the ship also ideal for carrying out secret rebel missions.

STAY BACK, STORMTROOPERS! **THIS SHIP HAS** DIPLOMATIC IMMUNITY!

Dual turbolaser turret

TANTIVE IV

Secondary turbolasers

Lower dual turbolaser

Control room windows

This is one royally great ship!

NEED TO KNOW

Model: *CR90 Corvette*

Length: *149m (489ft)*

Top speed: *950kph (590mph)*

Weapons: *Turbolaser turrets, laser cannon*

Made by: *Corellian Engineering Corporation*

Sensor rectenna

Engine turbines

Engine cooling vent

Airlock

 MISSION LOG

BATTLE OF SCARIF

The *Tantive IV* sped the Death Star plans away from Scarif before R2-D2 took them to Tatooine in one of the ship's escape pods.

BATTLE OF EXEGOL

After serving as a Resistance base on Ajan Kloss, the *Tantive IV* formed part of the historic fleet that brought down the First Order.

MISSING:
ONE TANTIVE IV ESCAPE POD

Last seen: Western Dune Sea, Tatooine

Reply: PO Box C3

 ## WHAT TO WEAR

The planet Alderaan was famous for its fashion. Be sure to wear a cool cape or a huge white helmet on any Organa family ship.

AS USED BY . . .

 **Senator Bail Organa**
Leia's adoptive father used the ship for official Alderaanian business during the Clone Wars.

 **Princess Leia Organa**
Leia used the *Tantive IV* to aid the Rebellion. Years later, she made it the flagship of the Resistance.

IMPERIAL LIGHT CRUISERS

They may sound like ships for a gentle holiday, but Imperial light cruisers mean serious business! These mobile command bases are just the thing if you have Empire-sized ambitions but you don't need something quite as big as an Imperial Star Destroyer.

OWNER'S TIPS

1. Don't get lost inside your own light cruiser. It's not a good look.

2. Remember not to say "Pew! Pew!" when firing the turbolasers.

3. Make sure visiting shuttles know which is the landing bay and which is the launch bay!

Turbolaser batteries

Forward launch bay

If you can read this, you're too close to my **turbolaser batteries!**

Light cruiser? Heavy bruiser, more like!

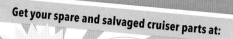

Get your spare and salvaged cruiser parts at:

GIDEON'S IMPERIAL REMNANT WAREHOUSE!

I'm not being a funny Moff when I guarantee you'll get money off!

When the Empire fell, so did our prices!
Extra discounts on your first order if you're secretly establishing the First Order.

NEED TO KNOW

Model: Arquitens-*class light cruiser*

Length: *380m (1,248ft)*

Top speed: *900kph (559mph)*

Weapons: *Turbolaser batteries, quad laser cannons, concussion missile launchers*

Made by: *Kuat Drive Yards*

Command bridge

Ion engine

IMPERIAL LIGHT CRUISER

Docking bay

SEE THE LIGHTER SIDE OF THE EMPIRE ON AN *Imperial Cruise!*

? OPTIONAL EXTRAS

Install extra charging points so that dark trooper droids can crew your light cruiser.

Four lights means this trooper is fully charged

Dark trooper droid

Hidden rocket boosters in feet

FIRST ORDER STAR DESTROYERS

The Empire's Star Destroyers were some of the biggest battleships the galaxy had ever seen. Then the First Order came along and made new ones that were almost twice as long! It's easy to see why this is the ultimate show-off's ship.

Turbolaser turrets

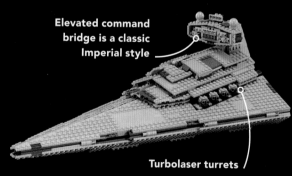

RESURGENT-CLASS STAR DESTROYER

TRY BEFORE YOU FLY . . .

For a vintage look (and easier parking) test out an Imperial Star Destroyer.

Elevated command bridge is a classic Imperial style

Turbolaser turrets

Performance
★★★★★

Handling
★★★★★

Usability
★★★★★

Overall
★★★★★

🔧 MISSION LOG

JOURNEY TO JAKKU
Resistance fighter Finn was still a stormtrooper aboard the Star Destroyer *Finalizer* when it came to Jakku in search of Luke Skywalker.

BATTLE OF EXEGOL
For the First Order's last stand, the *Resurgent*-class Star Destroyer *Steadfast* was joined by hundreds of newly built Sith Star Destroyers.

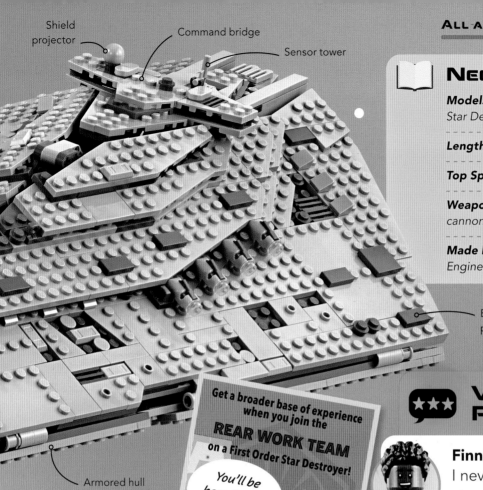

Shield projector

Command bridge

Sensor tower

Energy shield projectors

Armored hull plating

NEED TO KNOW

Model: Resurgent-*class* *Star Destroyer*

Length: 2,916 m (9,566 ft)

Top Speed: 775 kph (482 mph)

Weapons: Turbolasers, ion cannons, laser cannons

Made by: Kuat-Entralla Engineering

Get a broader base of experience when you join the
REAR WORK TEAM
on a First Order Star Destroyer!

You'll be here for the full stretch!

Live life at the sharp end when you join the
FORWARD WORK TEAM
on a First Order Star Destroyer!

It's the thin end of the wedge!

It's fun to play hide-and-seek on one of these!

VEHICLE REVIEWS

Finntastic2187
I never liked being a stormtrooper, but you do get a sense of general pride when you serve on board a Star Destroyer!

☆☆☆☆☆

General_Pryde
Really? I think that must be my aftershave, sorry.

DEATH STAR

When you've ruled out every other vehicle as too puny or just too pointy, the only thing to do is build yourself a big, round Death Star! It can't be beaten on size. Every vehicle we've checked out so far could fit inside one of these moon-size monsters.

Superlaser focus dish

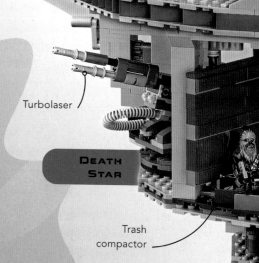

Turbolaser

DEATH STAR

Trash compactor

WHAT TO WEAR

The Emperor would argue that black best matches his favorite ship, but Palpatine's own Royal Guards have bright red uniforms.

AS USED BY . . .

The Emperor
Palpatine liked the first Death Star so much he had a second one built after the rebels blew it up. But then they blew that one up, too!

Grand Moff Tarkin
This Imperial governor ran the first Death Star as if it were his personal vehicle. On board, he even gave orders to Darth Vader.

Conference room

Prison level

Obi-Wan Kenobi at tractor beam controls

This one's a real all-rounder!

NEED TO KNOW

Model: *DS-1 and DS-2 Mobile Battle Stations*

DS-1 Width: *160 km (99 mi)*

DS-2 Width: *200 km (124 mi)*

Weapons: *Superlaser, turbolasers, laser cannons, ion cannons, missile launchers*

Made by: *Advanced Weapons Research*

VEHICLE REVIEWS

OrsonKrennicOK
I would not have spent so much on my Death Star if I had known they were going to bring out a Death Star II just four years later!

☆☆☆☆☆

Mon_Mothma
I've not actually been to the Death Star II, but I've heard bad things about it from many Bothans.

☆☆☆☆☆

Raise the Death Star II!

Recreate a slice of history with a contribution to the Death Star II Restoration Fund.

With your help, the currently ruined station on Kef Bir can become a vibrant community hub, flexible events space, conference center, and superweapon once again!

GLOSSARY

ASTEROID
A large rock in space.

ASTROMECH DROID
A type of small droid that fixes broken starships.

ATMOSPHERE
The gases that surround a planet.

BOUNTY HUNTER
A dangerous person whose job is to capture or even destroy another person for a fee known as a bounty.

CARBONITE
A special metal used to "freeze" objects or creatures in order to transport them across the galaxy.

CLONE
An exact copy of a living thing, made in a lab.

CLONE TROOPERS
Highly trained clones who fought for the Galactic Republic during the Clone Wars.

CLONE WARS
A three-year battle that took place across the galaxy, which led to the Empire's rise to power.

CUSTOMIZE
To build or change something to fit a person's individual wants or needs.

CYBORG
A person that is part human and part machine.

DIPLOMAT
A person who represents a particular place and helps negotiate peace.

DROID
A type of robot that is programmed to do particular jobs.

EMPEROR
The Sith Lord Palpatine who ruled the Empire.

EMPIRE
A powerful and cruel government that ruled the galaxy. It was led by the Sith Lord Emperor Palpatine.

ENGINEERING
The work needed to create and build something, such as a vehicle or a machine.

THE FORCE
The energy that flows through all living things. There are two sides of the Force—the light side and the dark side.

THE FIRST ORDER

An evil organization that formed after the Empire fell. They wanted to rule the galaxy.

FUGITIVE

Someone who has run away, usually to escape from danger.

GALACTIC REPUBLIC

The government that peacefully ruled the galaxy for many years. It fell when it was taken over by Sith Lords.

GALAXY

A huge group of stars and planets, which are held together by gravity.

IMPERIAL

Something that belongs to the Empire.

JAWAS

Small beings who live on the planet Tatooine. They search the deserts for scrap to sell.

JEDI

A member of the ancient Jedi Order, which promotes peace throughout the galaxy. Jedi study the light side of the Force.

JEDI MASTER

The highest rank for a Jedi who has done an exceptional deed.

LIGHTSABER

The swordlike weapon used by the Jedi and the Sith. Its powerful blade is made of pure energy.

PROTOTYPE

The first version of something, such as a vehicle, which is used to test a design.

REBEL

A person who rises up to fight against those who are currently in power.

RESISTANCE

The group that fought against the First Order to try to defend the galaxy.

SCAVENGER

A person who looks through junk in order to find something useful.

SITH

The group of ancient Force users who study the dark side of the Force.

SMUGGLER

Someone who moves certain goods from place to place, even though it is against the law to do so.

STEALTH

Moving in a way that makes it difficult to be detected.

STORMTROOPERS

Soldiers who worked for the Empire and then the First Order.

SUSTAINABLE

Not harmful to the environment.

TRANSPARISTEEL

A tough, see-through material used to make windows on ships.

INDEX

Penguin
Random
House

Senior Editor Tori Kosara
Designers James McKeag and Isabelle Merry
Production Editor Marc Staples
Senior Production Controller Lloyd Robertson
Managing Editor Paula Regan
Managing Art Editor Jo Connor
Publishing Director Mark Searle

DK would like to thank: Randi K. Sørensen, Heidi K. Jensen, Paul Hansford, Anders Hamilton Heidemann, Jens Kronvold Frederiksen, and Martin Leighton Lindhardt at the LEGO Group; Jennifer Heddle, Michael Siglain, and Leland Chee at Lucasfilm; Chelsea Alon at Disney Publishing; and at DK Matt Jones for editorial help, Julia March for writing the index, and Megan Douglass for Americanization.

First American Edition, 2022
Published in the United States by DK Publishing
1450 Broadway, Suite 801, New York, NY 10018

Page design copyright ©2022
Dorling Kindersley Limited
22 23 24 25 26 10 9 8 7 6 5 4 3 2 1
001–327059–May/2022

A catalog record for this book
is available from the Library of Congress.
ISBN 978-0-7440-5185-8
Library ISBN 978-0-7440-5186-5

Printed in China

For the curious

www.dk.com
www.LEGO.com/starwars
www.starwars.com